"*The Landfill Poems* combines fabular strangeness with a powerful evocation of material dispossession in the rural South. These seminal works come immediately to mind: *Shooting Rats at the Bibb County Dump, Deepstep, Battlefield, Child of God.* Cantrell distills elements of all these through the strength of his perceptual acuity and lively, off-kilter phrasemaking into a prayer for a world at the far edge of American mythmaking and exceptionalism. In its accumulative material warping, this book captures the texture of rural poverty. In its slicing, elliptical narratives, it brings us close to its subjects without judgment or caricature. "How down can a beast get?" "I fashion a feather from an entire sinus cavity to escape rust." "Ruin the quickest word you know on a good day." This is a beautiful and derelict sonnet sequence." — ***Tim Earley***

"*The cops comb her hair like ghosts* ends one in this amazing sequence of poems that wedge so much verbal power into the sonnet length that I find myself exclaiming: Wow, never a dull verbal moment here! Clay Cantrell in a *tour de force* of words writes a love story wrapped in a tangled hog-stomping mystery of a world that shifts between the sublime and the grotesque. I think of the French symbolists, Rimbaud, Verlaine, and their radical abandon into language, but this book carries the abandon to new, distinctly American levels." – ***John Bensko***

THE LANDFILL POEMS

Poems by
Clay Cantrell

First Edition
ISBN 978-0-692-79719-8

Cover and Interior Design: Lionel Ochoa,
Zence Imagery

Red Dirt Press
1831 N. Park Ave.
Shawnee, OK 74804
www.reddirtpress.net

Contents

For Evon & Cheryl

Some poems have been published in current or previous forms in the following publications:

Red Truck Review
The Journal
Deep South Magazine
Deluge

Sometimes our metal homes are worse than thatch
Or mud huts or hide tents, when the wind comes.

—James Whitehead

I.

Dorsal fin of death, moth of mother-scraps, pipe-
fittings fallen like scree. A miserable dung-heap, plastic
wrung with bone. The egret's neck awkwardly rests on milk jugs.
Cupid fills with lead the wasted straight-chairs
misers fling over nasty aluminum lips. My daddy can kill
more birds than your daddy. Antifreeze and water
kill off the whole Natchez Trace. Mister here's more trash
will you lend us biscuits? Methane burns a flame
stoned teenagers flee, trucks say we've been drunk
on self-image a hundred years. Send Tennessee's
organoid garbage trucks lest Friday come soon
lest fiberglass deter us detritus scoliosis beckons
the trail fucks up the slag pile, bilious a hundred
words written somewhere in the landfill's center.

II.

A soup can lays ripple to dust. Marrow jowls
are metal jowls, fabricated at dawn one cold January.
Grievers lay grime-slaked hands
on poor little mouths to hush us
when talk turns violet compacting violent I hope
tomorrow is better than today. The flies
light real bad accounting the tumor
as the sun warms blood, a redolent sickle
not unlike a tick's Lyme-ridden sore.
Who are we kidding? A tick does its job
the way an electric baler bales
limbs and souls in the earth.
The mountain of beer cans glints favorably.
Its majesty contemptuous, unspeaking.

III.

If any young darling sees the sewer
name her Lisa for the woods whence pray
young devils, knees sucked by mud-daubers
The ground waits to swallow squires and mischief alike
If the eyes resemble dandelions
showing signs of recent dilation or bloodshot
a swing-set made of eggshells
Lisa hears the lice-ridden drain ache
hears the smack of fist on temple
Like it or not Lisa scrambles eggs
and I fall to my knees like a stroke patient
watching her mold and season
my sun-blessed regalia, my lunch tray
Many nursing homes are called homes

IV.

Kern hoists feed bags full of twine.
His truck-bed of newspaper,
empty promises, spider-web
he is happy to break. His sister's
memory of a dead lover. A clump
of blighted elm boughs. Five days
hardly pays for the gas.
Deer hide dark with blood
staked with pastiche wordings.
An accrued death follows him.
Children's birth records, judgments,
cousins, bones make it in the pile.
The day he drives a mad heart
to its grave we might sell it.

V.

The soft surface of television says:
governor names Camden state garbage dump.
Lisa's face is cornbread
while the whole town wonders
if indeed the lord punishes
a thousand larcenies
a generation of lords
declaring law on rabies
they never even feel.
Lisa's face is cornbread
and I trap Styrofoam in the creek
to build chemical fires.
Looking up from TVs, kids
steal the ochre I so love.

VI.

I often sip beer
to pimp theories of God's drawstring.
Flood that engine with soul
or get off the shoulder. Shoulders
tell old lore of bent wicker
hair and brown spillage.
The first theories say trash
indicates life. The lime theories
admit trash deposits eat human
red ears and beer is built
in my own harsh image: sullen
lips and overalls completing
an overall ape shape. God's
garbage surrounds me.

VII.

I see the bone-yard of cattle maw. It hugs me, a fleck
itches a morning, smoke risen from heathen
collapsed meat, flank hulked on ribcage
flesh ferreted—coyotes reveal a secret jail—
ribs between face and the black crust-stains.
It is a kind of loss. Vacant eyes like dried-out bulbs.
Gnaw-marks on femurs. Go to town
and trowel bone more lovely than this.
I wake and think of petunia blisters
the nightly moldering. Nothing on scummy earth
sings different. Nothing sings flesh
down dunghills, the slow bath. I walk
quick in dawn-light to view fresh heifers.
A dirge of dirt. Happy fast dirt.

VIII.

I plod the driveway where dying is beige
stock, my thin calves striped like sunfish
cutting through a flood pool. It's okay
to throw my sister's diapers and toys
in the paunch creek. Her cancer fills us
with a hatred of garish lilies.
Days arrive and flee like dogs.
Sister takes a good picture, black
pinafore, old folks and cold rain.
I plot a trail to a bone yard, past kids
wallowing in pools, wearing abused cloth,
Goodwill sneakers rimmed with shit
and wet from frequent baptism.
Mud goodly dampens her eyelids.

IX.

Gully swill cramps my style, riles me,
eyes fixed on heavy bluegrass, a mitered sap
limping beer-canned miles between legs.
Its pockets of burnt rubber
drift oily waves to a new hangover
a news story of her smelted hands.
Tuesday nights it exiles the sonny boy
surveying curl-scrap littered yards.
Mother may I emulsify rawhide
may I Irish-up my offal?
Mired bonny lads cough births
out a wretched opera. Gully swill
wakes up alive and wormy
to cradle me in loamy palms.

X.

I wear rags on the moon. The surface is
crayon skin. A forlorn mayfly pealing
bank statements beneath peeled labels.
Cupped hands lift sideways fish
from a metaphorical ecosystem.
I wear an infernal satellite. Hands hang
like oaks scratching pocked dust.
It's been a mile since the gross bleeding
the exact second the radio cuts
and the voice of a rotten lover
feels closer than gravity.
If the grass burns break my fall.
I fashion a feather from an entire sinus
cavity to escape rust.

XI.

Ruin the crust of wispy porcelain head-stewed
Ruin a brown raindrop devoid of purpose
Ruin heads chopped off hillsides chop stone burials
Ruin rune spell death knell says hidy dalliance granny
Ruin sweet shell limed with ants liposuction mistake
Ruin cannon carbon monoxide cancer you want it
Ruin a lovely fingernail grimy one spring morning
Ruin a way of staring at antlions, ruin self-doubt
Ruin the clean snag of a hayfork, ruin in the knee
Ruin esophagus of ruined milk and honey floods
Ruin malty sermons piled like pack-mules
Ruin the quickest word you know on a good day
Ruin a verb that means soot-covered sucking
Ruin dragged down gravel, a heavy metal prayer

XII.

A storm of dead starlings somewhere
glitters. Bloodletting's a new business.
Come to the creek and feel plastic swill.
Tasty metal burned by rat's tonsure.
We are rain borne of celestial lashing, crimes
two sizes too small. The troughfuls. Pig feed's
the old business. Not too proud to eat
when stomachs too are junk. A storm
come to swish starlings somewhere,
a rubble-ring *de los muertos.* The eye retreads.
Forgets magic. We catch a capital gleam
in each other's eyes as pig feed bleeds out,
another apocryphal play thing. Wash it
down with metal in the poison creek.

XIII.

In moonlight wrecks the skin cries red
and Tony just cries. One spin of the truck
and the brute brakes. Then black paint
kisses Tony's torso real hard. It's scrap metal
mornings for outlaws who feel the sun
rising at dark, the menace of asphalt
cutting rugs down a holler. Switchback,
tree tops scratch our faces, a final
smack and Tony totters in scorched oil.
Skin sears thirty minutes until ether
pats the wounds. Flecks of blood
like pox on our cheeks. A week later
the junkyard pays three hundred bucks
for the hunk of metal that killed him.

XIV.

Kern burns a pool table. He satchels dregs
to and fro for the death-light shines full,
Thoth enraged to extend bright chair legs.
He whips his world with hard curses.
He shifts felt to knead the fire, nowhere
else to dump a head full of casualties
a clump of greens unclean till sifted, life
left back at the jukebox and pale flanks.
Kern don't fool the wide-eyed girlies.
Tonight corona of light glint or go out,
go right blight fire stack. Thought blinds
any cruel beat-down. He drags a mattress
to the wood pile's edge to weave evil
the alcoholic pentagram he draws.

XV.

All day dozers mine my life.
The drab edge of a quarry gifts
the highway new brilliance, vacant
blacktop always appearing dead
and lonely on drives home, dumb flame
lilting bright on western horizon.
No one thinks to blink when methane
eternal flares long as Christ, in kids'
nostrils, in my brain juice
when Lisa says she's incarcerated
by my own slow drifting away.
She asks why don't we pack for Biloxi
then *I say let's hide such sweet talk.*
We're too bored to have won the lottery.

XVI.

A pasty cloud beckons our filth.
We party all night on Main Street,
brushing mouths against others'
feckless motions. As cold a night
on the scabby knoll as I remember.
Cold zephyrs curl up our sleeves
and an outhouse aflame from diesel.
Everyone'll remember winter
was a dream of bored decades,
faces of the dead eroding
like unhappy pond scum.
Amen, Amen, Brother Kern,
sup deep your bottle of corn.
Burn now for us dog-gones.

XVII.

Lisa calls it home but I don't see
past stuffing-nests and springs. Metal
scuffs smile like land mines hidden
by a personal God, grief-shod greetings
to break the spirit. Lisa sniffles now
that God peek through bare limbs.
She says I better paint with blood
the dripping nude outlines I've toed
in dirt, sprayed on brick, dreamed.
She says it and she means we must
bleed teeth in repentance. Bleed's
the way to Lisa's ripped-up heart.
I don't see things in her lame vision.
I know she means to ignore me.

XIII.

The grate strikes midnight, hangs like a leper
the barrel's lifeline. It is blue life
that shakes within. Hate grows fat
eating sticks eating grime to court dates
raises us from tragic walks, heel kicks
grow divots on the sides of heads.
Sister says we look shiny in January.
I believe her. She grows hate, hours
get late early when beef jerky crumbs
pour down collarbones and plastic
beckons us fire-ward. It is a blue flame
dotes us. The hour eats like flesh
our long-sour endings. A hatchet bites
and hate burns before the barrel glow.

XIX.

The mattress sleeps on my thighs. Kicks
wake me. Time for a quick autumn and aches
quelled by drinking. Time hollow and wooden
pops down a face as the boys carry
playthings out the woods: a dirty pink purse,
empty gas can, shreds of grocery bags.
My heart goes shreds when eyes open.
They see me lying there, mud-slaked, beaten
and they hurry to beat me. I hope winter
comes hard in their cheeks. Time aches
for one more bowl of broth. One more cup
of corn by myself. The boys pop jake-leg
down the rock and my thighs ache so.
I do think the woods a good place to sleep.

XX.

We drink a rotgut
when the fire-ring says we drink too much
Beer cans and salt-licks yelp in our hearts
Rotgut says no alcoholic beverages
permeate our torsos like it does
my left hand shakes a paper bag
full and shattered by bottles, prescriptions
written to long-dead landlords, lo
and don't we get anxious around noon
parked outside the rifle-range, awake
to our own mistakes with money
Don't we cry before a moon face
appears in the apothecary's doorway
Shuck that clutch and backfire

XXI.

The sticky yolk of sex binds us after
our reveries, looking out the window
at the jackass toting an apple.
He's a depot he buries our marshes.
He quakes columns and rivers.
Our filial relationship to pain scrawled
Dint not the heady cabalistic log
fly methane and leachate, schools
of fish, mission bell lives. Carry apples
to far valleys of omission. Exhale.
In this way and others red discharge
of humans wafts over cobbles.
Sticky blocks of disposed blood
lope back up our dirty assholes.

XXII.

Mother, see the shredded
flesh on dry grass
Old dogs remind us
the body dies many times
We watch meteors
like silent missiles
My skin walks in sunlight
I press eyelids for you
The dogs poison the land
with moles and piss
I miss your steady hands
gently opening me
as I hand you figs
for the wasting away

XXIII.

Beg the ragman for ten dollars   Pay the moon pale
sick yellow a notion to smite   desire grows
a coughed up black lung   bile melting snow   desire is an ugly
twinkling of tears on rocks   it knows graveyards
It knows which saviors grow shame at the brow
Lie with me   in rapturous filth   rifles echo our crunchy
The highway sweeps callously along   I sweep my tendril
like a terrier bites ankles   like a meaty mass of shoulders
detached from thought   I comb the pimples the sex-groans
for signs of lace   here is my gossamer   its rapturous filth
cleft in a black chasm of longing   cleft a spasm of black
tears frozen and shuffling gravel   desire a coughed up
lung   a shrike of ugly notions ragmen spew forth
I pay a dark bower   a mile to graves   a gray sleep

XXIV.

Take a drink   o holy garbage can
thou jig is flowery   buttercup marrow crooked
I wake swimming   black rock to bowl of blood
where silver faces say   *tar the flesh tar the thorn forlorn soul*
Here is longitudinal crust   drink me   suck the end
off fractured knuckle   the face cries black tar
the face lies when wives apprehend other viscera
the face gapes long-intrusive waves of sorrow
scummed-out lawns drawn to kill cold shoulders
I wake drumming infant scowl looping hazardous
if you wallow dumb on sidewalk   eyeing the lock
We're so innocuous   I tell you over and over
Don't come around here waking up the kids
rheumy-eyed   mouth dripping crow blood

XXV.

Bless the dead pig   who remains wet   toil toll extant beast
oily cactus cracks the surface   sun bleeds on gristle distant as ever
distal as staked corridors   my life is a corridor smoking and stripped
of its distal parts   my sister and I   forking flesh thisaway like a spar-
kler above excess remains   she sits working catfish out the dumpster
She toils toll the extant beast many call *hunger*   many call *desire for*
God I mistake each black hole   they distribute cross scrubland ready
to pierce distended surfaces   distended ankles   tighten the calf
around un-distilled pinesap son and one day it'll feed you
The stake pierces smooth cartilage   it is cartilage of fresh death
We are creatures ugly in the creek   winsome to attract flies
to recognize black holes as originating from the bastard gloom
of Muscatine   very rare to perceive clean fish   her hand waves thither
perspiring a locus of torsion of scales strongly attached to eating

XXVI.

The jaw line recedes until it is like all the others.
An impish gaping of the mouth. Obsolete hairstyle.
Lisa's uniformity screams clean mulish eyes.
I am like her when I stir fish, pie, tongue
sandwiches, enjoy long-fluorescent bathrooms.
I am like her important death, her longing
for dinner mints. Our boredom never wanders.
She bared her jaw in nineteen eighty-four.
Lit up my brown bed like a crazed sun.
Raised a hand to my mouth. Her hair
goes fiery in mug shots. We say words like *sorry*
or *nothing much.* Today swallows us
in its mirror, its burnt money,
its endlessly disabled hoof-beats.

XXVII.

How down can a beast get?
How red hurt grass on the knees?
Tonight, I don't follow the drifting
kites, least of all on my back. The engorged
bestiality of bulldozers is empty
sans hilltops sans a friend at breakfast.
Sands glow luminous if left alone
for too many thousand tears.
This year purely dull, how down I get
in the back without your bullshit.
A hurt yearning for the backyard.
Too hard with heavy rot. I'm not looking
for a heart seriously pure red
or a tract of sand. I drift hard away.

XXVIII.

Vomit shares its sink with the party.
Most faces make no sense to Lisa.
Conversations come on like valium.
The party was boring long before midnight,
before rough lipstick, rough knuckles
cried on the shoulder of a crafty story
culled from loneliness, from dead industry.
Lisa claps knowingly at the small words.
Later scrolls are also boring.
Tomorrow the fulcrum will stretch
back into her swollen fingers
so that the whole party sees
how she swallows her candy.
The cops comb her hair like ghosts.

XXIX.

Pay attention to storms. They grin today,
when a straw-colored girl reeks of beat death,
a stained world beyond she would've greeted.
You tell her rain's a beat sight to behold.
You say you'll rain money come spring.
She solves your song, though, the one goes
like blue jays grating levees. The one
you keep yourself, cloud-worn winters,
thatched up charred chimneys, godless.
White afternoons, I'd nod in agreement
with your notions of cold silent living
but I suspect tire-tracks give way to her
not-unwarranted wonder at gambling men
from whom she longs shelter, death-cures.

XXX.

Gloom's the fusion of pebbles gloom's a sad tower
a wheel sawing counter to the sun, please paste plywood
plywood rotten all over concrete blocks, which scream
gloom's shot through with poison gloom's dry critter
long away the amino sky wonder gloom's ready to bloody
ready to pinch our nervous sidlings our shaky words
to one another when the moon bleeds and we are mute
gloom's the path once booted that's all briars and whist
wasps' sine wave lilting eave to block, it's our stable seat
our gesture to cracks, which menstruate, gloom's a live hoax
Gloom does not pretend truth, I know hates us, I know
our bodies softening response, gloom's a boring gray
we must stain though we'd rather say good to be here
Gloom's at the exact heart of gothic patches.

XXXI.

The hip chimes above the window wail
past midnight, while I toss on the fire
words like *needle* and *alone*. The mantle's
a starry beige, warmed from below but lost
in its own severity. Could you have guessed
me for a hermit? Snow splits gutters down
the seams when it freezes. A sandy crack
that wakes cracked walls from their age.
Tonight, I can't blame boredom or the blues.
Whole hours dissolve into the inert chill,
fastening me before an ashy, yawning hearth.
I know some hip cans, long-expired, touched
on their rims with dead wasps. This year,
I'm your lone ornament left, rotting.

XXXII.

Lean on the old. Taste her tired years in your jaw.
Morning scrawls memories of your wife on thin glass.
See her with a bible in the lamplight. The day her ankle
buckled by the pond. After the gray sky pierces
your eyelet window, the hillside looks unreal.
No more visits from faraway in-laws. No more
evenings watching the cat slink to her lap,
an ashtray filled with crinkled doctor's notes.
Lean away from the self. If your leg gives
no one will find you for days. Like her, advice
smiles and vanishes. Cold air is coming but why
do you care? The grass around the pond
hides the steep drop beyond. Dead sumac tassels
remind you of her unwashed copper hair.

XXXIII.

The sun draws you,
a crane fly to dull light, sin
the wild meadow you crawl.
Wed to this veiled day dejection
and thinking you'll never return
to your family's tract of pines,
now logged unrecognizably
in hazy memories you glean.
Your scene dismembers now
its motifs of frogs or skiffs
and precious limestone
scuttling the methane lanes
where broken losers
don't know the sun.

XXXIV.

Deer hide in burned carpet and limbs
broods down on us sarcastically. One
smoggy breath to draw sister and I
crawling like cretins to slaver, touching
fingers while rubber condoms flutter
in the distance. Brood down a storm
and hump our windows with ammonia.
Brood down from sky from god-sap
ether our thin starvation. Brood
in the window while sister and I
touch thighs and gymshorts, deer
hovering like ghosts. Then the turn
comes on like an underwhelming
buffett of fish, mush melon, flesh.

XXXV.

Lisa knows a battery charger's chug
though her battery no longer holds
workings of worth, her frown no secret.
Here waft the wasps and ammonia.
Here, a bloody rabbit, its entrails
hung from a dead tree, describing
how all trash likewise hangs around.
Scabs scuttle likewise her tough skin
and flashlights cattle like a bad forge
she leaves for entrails farthing shot.
Old engine won't turn though sperm
covers same ugly brown ground.
Scald this shit and slam dunk rabbits
if they don't know better, wafting.

XXXVI.

A drunk father scoots red ditches
and in five years dies eat up with scabs,
ammonia, and great clear ethyl Buddha
we've come to admire. Now ferrous
chairs stab their legs, pulp and fill dirt
recoiling, though their makeup is fake.
One of these incests will break time
or one scabby lad crushing self and sty.
The man was a cruel one, I say. Father's
ferrous vault grouts the ground some
way although we imbibe lame vapors
shot from methane vents and lye.
We don't care after long drunk vigils.
I doubt our dump world will die.

XXXVII.

Knees buckle and bleed the low scrub oak
which shall forever rise evil, this hot dirt
eroding putrid crows, Freon, fresh stomachs
of deer and inevitable ropes of copper.
I stagger I shiver though rot surrounds
and lament to Lisa the bag of dead cats.
I desire lyric love the rust barnacled trailer
once used for horses and dead shit
but I am searching a bed of unrecycled
paper to sleep to grab a thing wet and real.
Lisa disappears god vetoes our vetch
while vile milk sears on the bottom
of a five hundred degree metal box.
I stagger I shiver though rot surrounds.

XXXVIII.

Night hangs her eyes so pagan
and a bit of death in mine. On Fridays,
cheap wine slakes our throats, our pain.
We no longer count cans count rail bones
but verily eat cold cat food and discarded
greens although god gleams in the trash
and we mean to discard him a bit longer.
Today she slumped in metal, shaking
hands with a bit of death. Then night
broke her brain gleaming above me.
We no longer cast our dreams to days
or bad night when we nightly crash
glass down in the landfill's center.
A trash inside molds stony hearts.

XXXIX.

A nightmare clings to vile eyelids.
I'm on my back, white clouds parting,
yet rancid smells turn slow to blue.
I never killed the man who dirtied us
though his knell struck ten-year moans.
I want my inner dirt to wash away.
In my nightmare, he's bled by sheet
metal jagged, white skin ripping.
I want rancid juice drained in
his grave. I'm on my back, vile
and waiting. When dark falls,
it needles skin, drinks all blood.
Would I turned his dead ways.
Would I prayed gone this kin.

XL.

After methane and mattress mold
I scab Lisa, I scab rust boats and she's
a ghost—a wraith wrapped in dust.
Lisa, sister with darting-eye, you cry
the way prison meals cry, your willow
hair and tangled skin killing me again.
Kudzu hangs from the trailer's panels
to suffocate to chafe what limbs we
retain. Rusted box spring stays,
keeps Lisa company and boats
sit accepting of speed thoughts
and the ever-evil failings of night.
In the acidic stream we bathe nude,
scream up, and I scum my vitriol.

XLI.

A morn of brush and laminate water. I seek you,
speak you, press my wishes. I jerk my line its assisted living
and suck barn smells and the ring of black bottle glass
piled by miserly brass a chair for mister and old-shored.
Drag your piney fish bones, your flavor of ashy shoulder.
I am daydreaming again. I am the empty sky the empty
barrel sun rising burnt brown dealing with the limit.
Drag your reedy body on wood on ashy sofa and hold
me basking the terrible outdoors. The fish the herons
the kindled folks. See I seek your skin to kindle time
with me after peaks and valleys of wildlife jiggling.
Drag us through contaminate water. The rotted cake
of your belly. Fall out play the cards as melted glass
confines the long year. Break me thou empty skies.

XLII.

Jig skirts awkward on silver hook. God you hum
pelvic rot of god-brown berms like us. Are you a judge
are your feral tendencies fat with lard or the fish bones.
Here you scab in prisons crumbled by earth-maws, bad
ink stains we cairn you stay with us to guide our ankles.
Black-eye peas you old sore void feed us now and whiskey
is a knockout, squirms in these euryhaline brains. Sorry,
we'll rot together. Gar lurk rolling marsh weeds.
Call me when the diapers erode. Call me the silver hook
which depresses me you know I have issues. Looting,
our new fast food and breakup. Relationships are hard.
In the beginning, nothing happened, I swear. God scum
shat forth its carp and all the animals hit on me.
To riot awkwardly is worth a lot of money.

XLIII.

Lisa drinks river sludge. It's orange
forms hollow down in her insides.
I watch it grow and break her, it mirrors
my want for a relationship with the void,
awful empty of heart, which is full
of Tennessee's aluminum chunks. She
drinks aware of delicate furrows
that line her stomach, her soul. Orange
is the new weeping seeping defunct
we don't see coming. Lisa says her life
is at least close to me. We're a puzzle
unsalvageable in sickness and sickness.
Say we woke huddled on ugly chert.
Say we are rabies and poor folk.

XLIV.

Autumn grows shards we've naught to drink.
If toilet seats pitch malevolent pitch dozers
clang and the world hurts itself to sleep.
The dump never closes, workers die daily
of meth of mesothelioma onward knelt
to vastly metal grouts of fucking. Feel shards
bleed out autumn and the world goes to sleep.
What's been pitch plastic tools and dog skull
has been knifed through our carpals and veins.
Piss yellow spikes of goldenrod. Dandelions
ply the sky to draw them up. The dead
season, they're fast food and cooked bright-
yellow and black on our crusty fingers.
The dump never closes, hunger grows.

XLV.

Over & gone. Watching busted TV,
we fetch new skins beyond dark boughs,
jail hooch coming on strong. Kids
get over & gone. Too late and perch
won't chill overnight and we'll eat them
raw, bones & happy Lisa'll catch a buzz.
Too late. She falls across baling wire.
Skins a whopper, there's no rehab
shop, no radio sound. The damage
bounds beyond dark sidling glances
we cast at each other. Unfair mattress,
unfair raw fish, unfair sister loves.
Over & gone. Some doll parts remain.
The last transmission sent to none.

XLVI.

He steals life all gravel through, never visits
and curses rain out his indifferent sky. God
the water that runneth acidic the water holy
and poison. A broke clutch, a bathtub cut
through with silence. We're helpless now
drinking lye cursing sky cursing ourselves.
No book for this in the book-killing schools.
No skin touched in the barbed wire lessons.
Lisa washes holey dresses in orange creeks
and I scour banks, insulation, upturned
heaters for grub worms or smokehouse
salt, though usually we are given to fish,
gnawing the rib bones, sucking poison.
No book for this and he never visits.

XLVII.

Brothers while affections for mangy dogs.
They goed in the garden—is that what you say?—
and broke them spines them good turtle-shell
apples of evil and evil. I danced and laughed.
They ambled to me, speaking of new empires.
My south garden never was a garden at all.
Stones were thrown, no deathlore was careful.
After the first rock pile hurt us, earth quilted.
After the second rock pile, we knew to bury.
Real crypts, musty, they lied down together.
One for him, one for me, we better calm
the ire cause god and the devil divide dogs'
teeth the way weather opens the ribcage
and builds rock piles on boney empires.

XLVIII.

On Dry Branch Road, gravel speaks bloody
and neat. Red tractor parts rest, though wicked
they sire. Gravel goes *thick as fiddlers in hell*
and I hear the world growl like a dog, belches
eating and taken up by pride for curses fall
and often sire. Do not slay my self today
thus beggeth the Lisa who wishes her clothes
smelled like air fresheners at least who drinks
and wishes to erase her self. Do not speak
of bloody knee caps. Trash conspires. Gravel
becomes agitated when the boy won't leave
me alone. Carpet tacks on soft feet depress
me as long as I can remember and the nether
past dog hairs don't know our names.

About the Author

Clay Cantrell received an MFA in poetry at the University of Memphis. In 2015, He moved to Tulsa to pursue a PhD in Literature at the University of Tulsa. His poems have appeared or are forthcoming in *Sycamore Review, New Delta Review, Birdfeast, The Journal,* and elsewhere and his full-length manuscript, *Hermit, Wraith,* was recently a finalist for the St. Lawrence Book Award.